# THE NEED TO KNOW LIBRARY™

# EVERYTHING YOU NEED TO KNOW ABOUT
# SEXUAL ASSAULT

JEANA TETZLAFF

Rosen
YA™

New York

Published in 2018 by The Rosen Publishing Group, Inc.
29 East 21st Street, New York, NY 10010

**Library of Congress Cataloging-in-Publication Data**

Names: Tetzlaff, Jeana, author.
Title: Everything you need to know about sexual assault / Jeana Tetzlaff.
Description: New York : Rosen Publishing Group, Inc., 2018 | Series: The need to know library | Audience: Grades 7–12. | Includes bibliographical references and index.
Identifiers: LCCN 2017018440| ISBN 9781508176848 (library bound) | ISBN 9781508176831 (pbk.) | ISBN 9781508176862 (6 pack)
Subjects: LCSH: Rape. | Sex crimes.
Classification: LCC HV6558 .T47 2018 | DDC 362.883—dc23
LC record available at https://lccn.loc.gov/2017018440

*Manufactured in the United States of America*

# CONTENTS

INTRODUCTION.............................................................4

CHAPTER ONE
WHAT IS SEXUAL ASSAULT?.......................................7

CHAPTER TWO
SEXUAL ASSAULT AFFECTS EVERYONE .............................16

CHAPTER THREE
SEXUAL ASSAULT ON SCHOOL CAMPUS AND STUDENT
VICTIMS...................................................................26

CHAPTER FOUR
PROSECUTION AND POTENTIAL VICTIM TRAUMA..............37

CHAPTER FIVE
RECOVERY AFTER SEXUAL ASSAULT ...................................45

GLOSSARY ...............................................................53
FOR MORE INFORMATION.........................................55
FOR FURTHER READING...........................................59
BIBLIOGRAPHY.......................................................60
INDEX .....................................................................62

# INTRODUCTION

**W**hen someone is raped or otherwise sexually violated, that person is thrown into such emotional turmoil and trauma that it could have a negative impact on his or her life forever. Sex itself shouldn't be scary or horrible when consenting people are involved, but sexual assault is not sex. It's an act of violence. All sex acts require consent, whether verbal or nonverbal. Sexual assault can cause lasting trauma for the victim, as well as for those close to the victim.

Regardless of where you are, how you are dressed, or what you are doing, everyone deserves to be respected and safe. No one should ever be sexually attacked. Nor should anybody be made to feel responsible for having been sexually assaulted. Blame should always be on the perpetrator.

Victims of sexual violence are not just young women. People of all genders have faced some form of sexual assault. There are myths about this subject, and that plays into why it's not reported more often. Victims are often shamed or disbelieved. They can also be confused about what happened to them or unaware that any unwanted touching or groping is a form of sexual assault.

Victims also face the difficult decision of whether or not to press charges because the process of testifying

Victims of sexual violence will often have negative thoughts and feelings concerning what took place, which can have an impact on their loved ones, too.

in court can cause a victim to relive the experience again and again. And victims are often not believed and may be discredited in court. The popular misconceptions of what rape victims look like and how they should act—which are spread by the media and crime prevention efforts—don't help either. Many people believe that if a person was really victimized, she or he would scream and fight back. If a victim testifies that she or he didn't fight back, many in court and in the media ask if an assault actually occurred.

There are also many misconceptions about those who commit rape and other forms of sexual assault. It is often easiest to believe that only a stranger—a criminal with a record or other unsavory character—could commit such a crime. But in reality, only about 28 percent of sexual assaults are committed by a stranger.

The goal of the following passages is not to make you feel uncomfortable, but to help you to understand what sexual assault is and how it occurs, and to empower you with knowledge and support.

# CHAPTER ONE

# WHAT IS SEXUAL ASSAULT?

Sexual assault is a crime of power and control. It is not a crime of passion where the attacker has a strong desire for sex. It is never the result of the victim's actions but instead driven by the attacker's desire to dominate that person. There are certain social norms that also contribute to sexual assault and rape, like tolerating violence, using power over others, having a traditional mindset of toxic masculinity, wanting to control women, and being silent about violence and abuse.

Rape and sexual assault are criminal acts of violence. Rape is sexual intercourse (penetration) against a person's will. This also includes forcible sodomy, penetration with an object, or causing that person to penetrate herself or himself, against that person's will. Attempted rapes and verbal threats of rape are also sexual violence.

People of all genders can be victims of sexual assault. It can happen to anyone, including people with disabilities, regardless of race, age, social status,

Only a small percentage of sexual assaults are committed by strangers. Most sexual violence is committed by someone who the victim knows.

educational level, or gender. The majority of sexual assault goes unreported due to different social stigmas, like fear of not being believed or shame, just to name a few. According to a survey published by the Rape, Abuse, and Incest National Network (RAINN), about two out of three victims do not go to the police and only around 18 percent of reported assaults actually lead to an arrest. Other factors that prevented victims from coming forward include distrust of authorities and fear of blame.

# SEXUAL ASSAULT AND RAPE

Consent is important in any relationship between two people. Consent, or saying yes, should be freely given and not assumed. Giving in or being submissive as a response to fear or coercion is not consent.

There is a wide range of acts of violence that fall under sexual assault. It can take the form of unwanted verbal, visual, or physical contact. This includes being forced to perform sexual acts, rape, forcible sodomy, forcible object penetration, kissing, fondling, marital rape, unwanted sexual touching, sexual contact with minors, incest, and any unwanted or coerced sexual contact.

The fondling/groping could be anything from grabbing buttocks to touching breasts, or even just an unwanted hug—it's whatever makes you feel violated. Your personal space should always be respected.

Perpetrators may use emotional coercion, psychological force, or manipulation to coerce a victim into nonconsensual sex. Some offenders will use threats to force a victim to comply, such as threatening to hurt the victim or his or her family. These offenders may use other intimidating tactics to pressure the victim.

You have the right to a healthy, respectful relationship. Sex within a relationship should be consensual. It can be as simple as, "Are you OK with this?" and then waiting for a clear answer of "yes" or some form of nonverbal consent.

Respect for one another plays an important role in any relationship, and no one should ever be coerced into a sexual act. This includes non-mutual sexting and online sexual harassment.

## ALCOHOL

Alcohol can play a significant role in sexual assault. Binge drinking, in particular, has sometimes been tied to it. Binge drinking is when males consume five or more alcoholic drinks or females consume four or more alcoholic drinks in two hours' time. Women's bodies metabolize alcohol differently than men do, so women tend to get intoxicated faster.

Some experts recommend avoiding alcohol as a preventive measure. However, others point out that rapists are responsible for rape and it shouldn't matter if a victim has been drinking or not. While at a town hall meeting, Ohio governor John Kasich answered a college freshman's question about his plans to improve campus safety regarding sexual violence. He called for increased access to rape kits plus places where victims can go and have confidential reporting along with an opportunity to pursue justice after the victim has had time to reflect on it. According to an article in *Salon*, Kasich had some additional advice on avoiding rape: "Don't go to parties where there's a lot of alcohol." Although Kasich meant well, it still came off as casually blaming the victim since he did not have advice for the young men who were in the audience. The message of prevention should include a discussion about awareness while socializing. The focus shouldn't be just to avoid drinking or parties.

Ohio governor John Kasich was accused of victim blaming after some advice he gave to victims during a town hall meeting.

Many state laws say that a person who is impaired due to the influence of alcohol or drugs is not able to consent to sexual activity. It is criminal for someone to deliberately use alcohol as a means to subdue someone in order to engage in nonconsensual sexual activity. Victims are never to blame regardless of whether they were drunk or not.

# SEXUAL HARASSMENT

Sexual harassment is any unwanted or coerced sexual contact. It can include kissing, fondling, groping, requests for sexual favors, and other verbal assaults that are sexual in nature. Sexual harassment can occur in the workplace, in school, on campus, and in the military. It can also take place on the street and in public settings. Anyone can be a victim of sexual harassment.

Harassment is severe, persistent, or pervasive behavior that interferes with, limits, or deprives a person from participating in or benefiting from education or employment programs and/or activities. It can affect an individual's employment and work performance. It may also create an intimidating, hostile, or offensive environment. The harasser may be a fellow student, a staff member, a supervisor at work, a higher-ranking military personnel, an employer, a fellow employee, or the agent of an employer. Someone from another business that is associated with your employer can also be an offender.

Sometimes, telling the offender "Don't touch me" or "Leave me alone" may be enough to stop the harassment. But if the harassment continues, then write down specific events that happened, including where and when. If the harassment happens at school, report it to a teacher, guidance counselor, or school administrator. At work, a complaint can be filed with the human resources department (if one exists), if you don't feel comfortable going to your supervisor. Employers are encouraged to take steps to prevent sexual harassment from occurring. They should provide sexual harassment training to their employees and establish an effective complaint or grievance process.

Alcohol is commonly used in drug-facilitated sexual assaults. By itself, alcohol slows reflexes and can impair the victim's ability to recognize a dangerous situation. It can also contribute to an anything-goes environment, which can include rape by individuals or groups of men. When it comes to dealing with intoxication and sex, there will be incomplete memories and differing perceptions of intent and consent.

## DATE RAPE DRUGS

Even a single drink (alcoholic or not) can be drugged by an attacker. The term "date rape drugs" refers to substances that an offender gives the victim before committing sexual violence. That offender can be a stranger, a date, or a friend. There are a variety of substances that can be used to immobilize a person. Prescription drugs such as sleep aids, anxiety medications, muscle relaxers, and tranquilizers can render the victim quickly unconscious when taken with alcohol. Club drugs such as GHB, Rohypnol, and ketamine (also called Special K) have no color, taste, or smell. They can be easily slipped into drinks. Because of the sedative properties of these drugs, victims often have no memory of an assault, only an awareness or sense that they were violated.

According to RAINN the warning signs of having been drugged are:

- Difficulty breathing
- Nausea

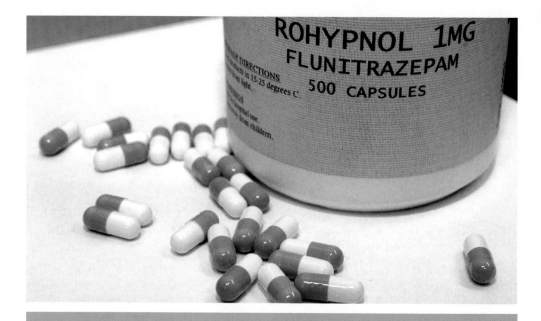

Rohypnol, also known as roofies, is a drug often used to immobilize a victim before an assault.

- Feeling drunk when you have consumed no or only small amounts of alcohol
- Loss of bowel or bladder control
- Sudden body temperature changes that make you sweat or make your teeth chatter
- Sudden increase in dizziness or disorientation
- Waking up with no memory, or missing parts of memories

Drugs generally leave the body within twelve to seventy-two hours. That means that urine and blood tests need to be done immediately, usually as part of a sexual assault forensic exam, to detect if a victim was drugged.

# MYTHS AND FACTS

According to Georgetown Law, the US Department of Justice Office on Violence Against Women compiled the following myths and facts of sexual violence.

**MYTH:** Most sexual assaults are committed by strangers.

**FACT:** Most acts of sexual violence are done by someone the victim knows. Two-thirds of victims from ages eighteen to twenty-nine had a prior relationship with their attacker. Most often it's a partner or ex-partner, classmate, friend, acquaintance, coworker, fellow soldier, or superior officer.

**MYTH:** Rape can be avoided if people stay away from dark alleys and other "dangerous" places.

**FACT:** While it's a good thing to avoid dark alleys or "dangerous" places, rape and assault can occur at any time and in any place. According to a report based on FBI data, 70 percent of rapes reported occurred in the home of the victim, the attacker, or another person.

**MYTH:** Only young, attractive women are assaulted.

**FACT:** Sexual assault occurs to all genders, all ages, all races, and people with disabilities. The attackers choose people whom they perceive as weak and vulnerable and assert their power over them.

# CHAPTER TWO

# SEXUAL ASSAULT AFFECTS EVERYONE

Teens and young adults are at a higher risk than the rest of the population, but rape and sexual assault can still take place anywhere, to anyone, at any-time—on the street, in your home, on campus, in the military, or on the job. Most sexual assaults are committed by someone the victim knows and has a relationship with. The person who commits acquaintance rape could be a date, a classmate, a neighbor, a friend's significant other, or any person the victim knows. The term "date rape" is sometimes used in place of "acquaintance rape."

In other instances, the victim may not know the attacker. This is called stranger rape, and it can happen in a few different ways. During a blitz sexual assault, an unknown attacker quickly assaults the victim without prior contact. This usually occurs in a public place at night. Before a contact sexual assault, the offender will spend a short time trying to gain the trust of the victim. The attacker will then use any means to lure the victim to a car or place where the sexual assault will occur. When an offender

An innocent date ought to be fun and respectful, too, so your companion should never expect more from you than what you are comfortable with.

invades the victim's home to commit sexual violence, it is a home invasion sexual assault.

## NO GROUP OF PEOPLE IS SAFE

No group of people is safe from sexual violence. People of every race, religion, age, sexual orientation, gender, and social class have dealt with sexual assault. According to the National Intimate Partner and Sexual Violence Survey (NISVS), conducted in 2010, the percentage of people of different sexual orientations who reported sexual violence other than rape during their lifetimes is as follows:

- Heterosexual men: 20.8 percent
- Heterosexual women: 43.3 percent
- Gay men: 40.2 percent
- Lesbian women: 46.4 percent
- Bisexual women: 74.9 percent
- Bisexual men: 47.4 percent

Nevertheless, members of some groups are more likely to be sexually assaulted than others. For example, RAINN reports that Native Americans are twice as likely to be sexually assaulted than non-Native Americans. Sexual assault is also a major problem in the transgender community. According to RAINN, 21 percent of transgender or gender-nonconforming college students have been sexually assaulted. In comparison, 18 percent of non-TGQN (transgender, genderqueer, nonconforming) female students have experienced a sexual assault, while 4 percent of non-TGQN male students have.

## WHAT TO DO IF THINGS GO TOO FAR

Perpetrators use guilt and intimidation to pressure their victims into situations of sexual violence. According to a *Campus Safety* magazine statistic, one in five female high school students is physically and/or sexually abused by a date. Whether you are out on a date or just hanging out with a friend, your personal space should always be respected. Here are some tips—several of which come from RAINN—to keep you safe if your date becomes questionable and you are suddenly at risk:

**Know that this isn't your fault.** The person who is pressuring you is the one responsible, not you.

**Trust your gut.** Listen to your gut reaction if you don't want to do something. Stick to what feels right and what you are comfortable with.

**Use a code word.** Come up with a word or phrase with friends or family that means, "I'm uncomfortable," or "I need help." This will let you get help without alerting the offender.

**It's OK to lie.** To avoid angering or upsetting this person, you can lie or make an excuse to create an exit. Don't feel obligated to stay in a situation that is uncomfortable, scary, or threatening. Even going to the bathroom can create an opportunity to get away or to find help. Whatever you need to say to be safe is OK.

**Think of an escape route.** What would you do if you had to leave quickly? Check out where the windows, doors, and other exits are. Look for other people who might be able to help you. Where can you safely go?

**Use verbal or physical resistance.** Fight back and yell loudly or swear in the perpetrator's face. If you know any tactics from self-defense, use them.

**Don't plead with the person to stop.** Demand that he stop or make a scene if you have to.

Trust your instincts. If you feel threatened by a date, even if it's someone you know well, don't be afraid to get away from the situation.

**Don't be polite or afraid to hurt their feelings.** It's OK to tell someone, "Don't touch me," or "Stop it. I don't like this," if you don't want to be touched.

Identify risky situations. Don't go alone to a party or bar and always keep whoever you went with informed on where you are going, no matter if it's just going to the bathroom. Don't get isolated. Instead, stay near groups of people who would be able to hear you if you were attacked. Trust your instincts and intuition and do whatever you think is most likely to keep you safe and alive.

## SUPPORTING SOMEONE WHO HAS BEEN ASSAULTED

If someone you know is sexually assaulted, there are a number of ways you can help out and be supportive. The website Best Colleges recommends the following:

- Help the victim get to a safe location.
- Tell the victim he or she is not to blame for the attack.
- Be supportive as you listen to the victim and believe him or her.
- Take detailed notes about the incident if you saw part of the attack or the assailant.
- Take the victim to get medical help and to meet with someone who specializes in sexual assault trauma.
- Encourage the victim to go to counseling sessions and support groups.
- Be aware of the survivor's emotional and physical status. Victims of sexual violence are at a higher risk for depression, PTSD, eating disorders, and suicide.

## THE VICTIM'S RESPONSE WHEN ATTACKED

Everyone reacts differently when dangerous situations occur. Some may struggle or put up a fight. Others may feel that fighting or resisting may make the attacker angry, resulting in more severe injury. There is no "correct" way to respond to an attack. Some victims may fight back and run away. Others may freeze. Freezing

During a violent act, a victim may freeze, feeling unable to protect herself and get away from her attacker.

is a documented neurobiological condition where a person cannot move in extremely fearful situations. It is uncontrollable and not something a person decides to do. Some victims will completely disconnect during the rape and think of other things. Freezing and withdrawing are not forms of consent. Unfortunately, the victim is all too often asked why she didn't fight back when rape cases go to court. No victim should be held accountable for what happened to her based on her action at the time of the attack.

## DEALING WITH SEXUAL ASSAULT: TWO DOCUMENTED CASES

The Netflix documentary *Audrie & Daisy* tells the stories of two girls who faced difficult circumstances after they were sexual assaulted. Their experiences illustrate how sexual assault can poison the lives of its victims.

## THE AUDRIE POTT CASE

High school student Audrie Pott was sexually assaulted by three teen boys after she passed out from drinking

Audrie Pott's mother, Sheila, is seen here with a portrait of her daughter, who committed suicide after she was sexually assaulted at a party.

at a friend's party. In one of the bedrooms, the teens used markers to draw on her body before one of them sexually assaulted her while another took pictures. The next day, Audrie had no memory of what had occurred so she questioned her friends and found out who had assaulted her. In the week that followed, the pictures of her went around at school and on social media. Audrie begged the boys to take down the photos, but they refused. She felt her reputation was ruined forever and that her life was over. By the end of that week, her mother got a text from Audrie saying "can't do this anymore." That same afternoon when Audrie got home from school, she hanged herself in the shower.

## THE DAISY COLEMAN CASE

Daisy was fourteen when she was raped by seventeen-year-old fellow student Matthew Barnett—a friend of her older brother. Daisy and her friend Paige had been drinking in her room when she received a text from Barnett, inviting her over. Her brother was home, asleep, when this occurred. The girls met up with Barnett and three of his friends, who were also drinking. Paige was sexually assaulted by one boy, and after Daisy passed out, she was raped by Barnett. Then on that cold January night, the boys took the girls home and left an unconscious Daisy lying out in the front yard. When Daisy was found the next morning, she was near comatose from alcohol poisoning and very cold. While her mother was drawing a bath with cool water to try and warm Daisy slowly, she noticed the redness when undressing Daisy. She immediately took her to the emergency room and had a rape kit done. The sheriff was called, and an investigation started.

The Monday after the incident, Daisy returned to school and everything changed. During the investigation, she couldn't talk about the assault case but she had to deal with name calling, like "slut" and "whore." Former friends refused to stand up for her. After the charges were dropped, Daisy endured verbal attacks at school and on social media. Daisy hated going to school and going out in public. The verbal attacks continued along with threats. She started believing what was said, that she was a bad person and that it was her fault. The family endured vandalism to their home before it was burned to the ground and her mother lost her job due to the case. The family moved to another town, an hour away, just to keep everyone safe.

Daisy internalized the negativity until it took her into a dark place. She tried to overdose on pills several times. She dyed her hair black and burned herself. She felt alone and posted on social media things like, "The pressure to be perfect is much stronger than the love in this world" and "Out of all the things...why did I become this?..."

# CHAPTER THREE

# SEXUAL ASSAULT ON SCHOOL CAMPUS AND STUDENT VICTIMS

B eing on a college campus can give a student a sense of security. That feeling of knowing each other and watching out for one another may make some students less alert to what is going on around them. Some perpetrators will take advantage of this feeling of security to commit acts of sexual violence. According to RAINN statistics, 11.2 percent of all students experience rape or sexual assault. More than 50 percent of campus sexual assaults occur in the fall.

Sexual assault on campus often goes unreported. Student victims choose not to come forward due to a multitude of feelings and beliefs. They may experience fear or shame, or they may blame themselves. Some survivors are in disbelief about what happened or aren't sure that a crime occurred because they knew and trusted the offender. Others worry that they will be viewed differently by other students and staff, that they will not be taken seriously if there is no evidence (such as a rape kit), or that the offender will go unpunished if a claim is brought forward to the school.

College campuses are meant to give students a sense of security, but one in five college students will be victims of a sexual assault.

After the growing national concern, the Obama administration launched the "It's On Us" initiative in 2014. Its goal was to focus on the prevention of and response to sexual assault on college campuses in the United States. As a result, universities and colleges are working to improve support services for victims.

## CAMPUS ENVIRONMENT CONCERNING RAPE AND SEXUAL ASSAULT

Under Title IX of a US law called the Education Amendments of 1972, people are protected from sex discrimi-

# SEXUAL ASSAULT STATISTICS ON CAMPUS

*Campus Safety* magazine reported the following statistics about campus rape in 2012:

- Between 20 percent to 25 percent of college women experience completed or attempted rape.
- In 2.8 percent of completed rapes and 35 percent of attempted rapes, victims were on a date with the offender.
- College freshmen and sophomore women are at greater risk of sexual violence than are upperclassmen. Eighty-four percent of the women who reported experienced sexual assault during their first four semesters on campus.
- Men in fraternities have been identified as more likely to commit sexual assault than non-fraternity members.
- College men who participated in aggressive sports (football, basketball, wrestling, and soccer) used more sexual coercion in their dating relationships then men who had not.
- Students living in sorority houses are three times more likely to be raped than students living off campus. Those living in on-campus dormitories are 1.4 times more likely to be raped than their counterparts who live off campus.
- In one in three assaults, the offender was intoxicated.
- Forty-three percent of the sexual violence involved alcohol consumed by the victims, and 69 percent involved alcohol consumed by the attacker.

nation in education programs and activities that receive federal funds. If colleges that receive federal funds (as most colleges do) refuse to comply, they can lose that funding. Because sexual assault and sexual harassment limit the ability of students—particularly female, non-straight, and transgender students—to get an education, they qualify as forms of sex discrimination. Title IX requires colleges to protect every student's equal right to an education by addressing all allegations of sexual assault and sexual harassment.

Many colleges direct this type of allegation through campus security. According to RAINN statistics, 86 percent of campus law enforcement agencies can

Title IX protects every student at colleges and universities, regardless of gender, from sex discrimination, which includes sexual assault and sexual harassment.

make an arrest outside of the campus grounds. The same percentage has a rape prevention program. Seventy-two percent of campus law enforcement departments have a staff member who specializes in survivor response and assistance.

Colleges deal with sexual assault reports differently than the police do. While a college can suspend or expel a sexual offender, it does not have the authority to send a person to jail for sexual assault. For that, the person who was sexually assaulted would need to go to the police and then the assailant would need to be tried and found guilty of the crime.

After a sexual assault, a survivor may seek to get justice both by going to the police and by reporting the assault to school authorities. In cases of sexual assault, college administrators and police work independently of each other. The police do their own investigation of the case. If physical evidence from the victim is not collected early in the process, then it will be hard to pursue criminal action. Physical evidence is crucial in police investigations.

However it is not unusual for survivors of campus sexual assault to report it to campus authorities, but not to the police. College administrations can protect students by acting quickly to suspend or expel offenders. If the victim went through the local police, then it could take years before the offender, if found guilty, would face prison time. Colleges can take other steps to protect victims, too, such as changing either the victim's or the assailant's dorm room or class schedule. They can offer counseling or academic accommodations (such as extensions on papers or make-up exams) to students who have been sexually assaulted.

Colleges and universities may also offer avenues to pursue justice when the law does not. For example, some state laws don't cover sexual violence if the attacker is a female or if the victim and offender are the same sex. Some state laws won't even recognize men as victims of sexual assault.

Additionally, some survivors feel that campus reporting is their only option because they fear skepticism and abuse from police, prosecutors, or juries. They may be aware that most reported rapes do not lead to an arrest, much less a conviction. While the outcome of reporting a sexual assault to campus authorities isn't assured either, schools don't need the same level of proof to take disciplinary steps against people accused of sexual assault as the police and courts do.

Unfortunately, this has led some schools to discourage victims of sexual assault from taking their cases to the police. To make matters worse, many colleges aren't as responsive as they should be to reports of sexual assault.

## NOT COMING FORWARD

A high percentage of US campus rapes go unreported. Victims don't come forward for a variety of reasons. One issue is the fact that college staff are often not properly trained to deal with sexual assault and rape. Sexual assault survivors also may not want to put themselves though the painful experience of adjudication, as hearings are known. On campus, after a victim reports sexual assault, he or she must go in front of a panel hearing done by the school's administration. The victim is asked questions and has to share the horrific details of the attack. Some students feel this process is unjust since the victim must go before a panel, where the victim's identity and behaviors will be questioned and held against an idealized standard. The media portrayal of what a victim looks like and how she or he should act might be a factor in how the administration views the case, and if there isn't enough evidence, the offender will go unpunished.

Students who are sexual assault victims will have different reactions, depending on their experience. Some will be in denial or won't recognize the assault or rape that happened, especially if it's by someone they know, like a friend or dorm mate. Here are some of the reasons why victims choose silence:

**Self-protection:** These individuals don't want their perception of themselves to change or be defined by the sexual violence. Some victims fear not being believed if they press charges. They may have showered after the rape, destroying any physical evidence needed for a rape kit. Perhaps they couldn't provide evidence that force was used in the attack.

**Protection of the perpetrator:** Some victims may try to protect the offender, if it's someone with whom they have previously been close.

**Protection of social groups, such as student workers, Greek communities, and athletic teams:** If rape or assault occurs within a certain group of people, there may be pressure on the victim to not press charges and keep it quiet. Athletic teams and fraternities often hold significant power and privilege on campus. Their members can impact the culture of the school in significant ways for better or worse. Whatever the attitudes, it can influence the nature of the campus community in safety and in being supportive or not.

**Protection of family and friends**: Sometimes the victim doesn't want to burden loved ones with the knowledge of the attack.

In *Campus Sexual Assault: College Women Respond* by Lauren Germain, one victim who was interviewed shared that after she had been raped at a fraternity party, she was pressured by other sorority members not to report the attack since the perpetrator was someone they knew. But on a different campus, when another victim was interviewed, her experience was of getting support from her sorority sisters after she was sexually assaulted at a party. They encouraged her to report it and then continued to be there for her.

## PUNISHMENT ON CAMPUS

On campus, some victims don't press charges because they are worried about how the panelists chosen

# SEXUAL VIOLENCE IN RELATIONSHIPS

Sexual violence is never okay in intimate relationships. Victims often won't recognize the danger until the assault happens. According to Best Colleges, victims must take steps to leave a sexually abusive relationship.

- **Contact a support line:** Don't be afraid to contact a support hotline for assistance.

- **Don't blame yourself:** Don't feel trapped or shamed if you find yourself with someone who is sexually abusing you. That person is at fault for his or her actions.

- **List safe places:** Have a safe place where you can go to if you feel threatened. This could be a campus counseling center, a trusted friend's place, or a survivors' shelter.

- **Document hostile communications:** Save threatening messages sent from your partner. This includes voice messages, emails, IMs, and texts that can be useful to show a history of assault when you talk to counselors or authorities.

- **Get counseling:** Most college campuses have counselors who can help with relationship assault and domestic violence.

- **Call the police:** If you are threatened, go to a safe place and call the police immediately.

by college administrators will interpret the incident. Others feel pressing charges is a high-risk endeavor with a low chance of actually leading to justice or protection for themselves or other students. Any sexual violence case hearings that are done on campus are confidential. The common perception is students are rarely found guilty or responsible.

If the perpetrator is found guilty after the adjudication process, the punishment varies depending on the school and the type of assault. The penalty can be minor, as in making the accused write an apology letter or a summer suspension can be given. Some schools may defer to the survivor, giving her or him penalty options to choose from. This alternative puts an unfair burden on the victim, where she or he may feel more responsible for what happened. Other schools can have "mandatory minimum" sentences where the suspension imposed must be at least one year or until the victim graduates, whichever one is greater. The most serious disciplinary action is expulsion.

# 10 GREAT QUESTIONS TO ASK A STUDENT COUNSELOR

1. Is there an understandable policy that prohibits sexual violence?
2. Can students report assaults anonymously?
3. Does the college provide sexual violence programming for all new students and ongoing programming throughout the year?
4. Are there support and resources for a sexual assault survivor, such as an advocate and mental health counseling?
5. Does the campus have a sexual assault response team that coordinates with professionals like law enforcement and medical officials?
6. How transparent is the judicial process?
7. Will the victim be held responsible for violating student conduct codes?
8. What is the punishment for sexual offenders?
9. Does the school enforce no-contact orders?
10. Do students have a real voice in the process, and who are those students?

# CHAPTER FOUR

# PROSECUTION AND POTENTIAL VICTIM TRAUMA

Rape prosecution can be a drawn-out and painful process. It could take months before anything is done if the assault occurred on a campus, if charges are brought at all. In the case of Tucker Reed, who was raped by her boyfriend in 2010, she was able to obtain a recording of her then-ex-boyfriend confessing to the crime. However, charges were never brought against Reed's attacker by the University of Southern California, despite the confession. Reed's alleged rapist went on to countersue her for libel.

Going to the police and filing charges through the court system could take months to several years. During this time, victims have no idea what to expect or what the outcome will be. The case against alleged rapist Brock Turner, who sexually assaulted an unconscious female student (who chose to remain anonymous throughout court proceedings), in January 2015, resulted in a six-month sentence. Turner served three months and was released.

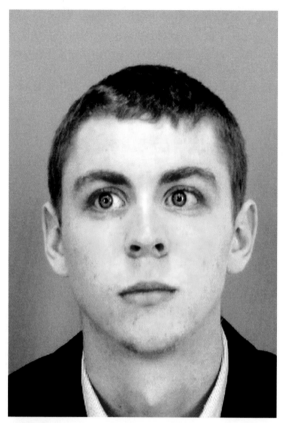

Brock Turner served three months of a six-month sentence for the on-campus assault of a 22-year-old woman.

# PROSECUTION BY THE STATE

Since the legal system can be intimidating and confusing, victims must have courage if they want justice and the offender off the street. But they don't have to do this alone. Most communities have rape crisis centers that provide advocates, counselors, and other valuable resources as you move through the legal system.

It is up to the state to prove the victim was sexually assaulted and if the rapist used force or threatened force against that person. The legal process is not easy, so the victim will need an attorney, known as a prosecutor. It could take a few months to several years depending on how the assailant pleads, guilty or not. The victim will have to be prepared to think and talk about the rape, to go through the events over and over. It is critical to have support of friends, family, or counselors through this difficult time.

The victim will endure medical examinations and possibly psychiatric examinations. Treatment by the defense attorney, who represents the rapist, during depositions and at trial could be harsh, potentially painting the victim as a liar and accusing her of doing this for attention. The victim's body and identity will be called into question: What was she doing before the attack? What was she wearing? How forcefully did she say no? Was the physical evidence on or inside her?

Family, friends, and others the victim shared her story with may be called to testify, not only about what was said, but about their perceptions of the victim and the victim's behaviors.

# WHAT TO DO IF YOU'RE SEXUALLY ASSAULTED OR RAPED

If you are the victim of sexual violence, there are some steps you should take, if possible, to protect yourself

**Get to a safe place:** Run from your attacker to a safe place that has people around and call for help. A campus health center is a good location if you are at school, or go to a nearby friend's or family member's home.

**Don't wait to report it:** Do not shower or change clothes no matter how dirty or tainted you may feel. Showering, brushing teeth, and changing clothes can destroy the physical evidence.

# FALSE CLAIMS

It is estimated that only 2 percent of rape claims are false. A false claim is a reported crime to law enforcement where an investigation proves it never occurred.

According to the National Sexual Violence Resource Center (NSVRC), victims face challenges when reporting sexual assault. It doesn't help when there is a culture to blame victims along with the myth that false rape claims are a common problem. There are some in law enforcement who may not have had the right training on sexual violence and could have the perception of victims being phony, inconsistent, or untrue. Rape victims should be believed and supported until it is proved that nothing occurred.

Some believe that an accuser may use the serious charge of rape for revenge, to gain an upper hand, or to otherwise harm an innocent person.

The determination for a false claim is if the evidence establishes that no crime was committed or attempted. According to NSVRC, the FBI and IACP (International Association of Chiefs of Police) have issued guidelines to help identify false reports:

- Insufficient evidence to proceed to prosecution
- Delayed reporting
- Victim not cooperating with investigators
- Inconsistencies in victim statement

**Advocacy:** Call the National Sexual Assault Hotline (800-656-HOPE) to help guide you in getting an emergency advocate and help.

**Contact authorities and go to the hospital:**
Call 911 or the police. Seek medical attention as soon as possible. Valuable evidence will be gathered by a nurse or doctor for a rape kit. A rape kit will find fibers, hairs, saliva, or semen that the attacker may have left behind. The doctor will also document injuries and collect DNA evidence: hair, skin, and bodily fluids.

**Emergency contraception and STD testing:**
Pregnancy can be prevented by taking Plan B up to 120 hours after an attack. Ask to be tested for potential infections that can be transmitted through sexual intercourse.

**Write down everything you can remember as soon as possible**: To protect ourselves, memories of traumatic events are often suppressed. While it's still fresh in your mind write down what happened.

**Have a friend or rape crisis counselor with you throughout the process:** Reach out to those around you for support.

You can ask the state for financial assistance to help obtain services—medical examinations and crisis counseling.

Many medical professionals are trained to help the victims of sexual assault by collecting evidence and documenting injuries.

Many victims may hesitate on labeling rape or sexual assault right after it happens. They may be in shock or have general difficulty calling it for what it is, rape or sexual assault. They might be concerned about the legitimacy of their experiences in relation to how the labels are applied. Is the level of force used or the severity of injuries considered rape? Even if the victim is questioning what happened, if it was forced and unwanted, it's sexual assault. The victim should seek help immediately.

## DAISY COLEMAN'S COURT CASE

In the case of Daisy Coleman, the prosecution's investigation took months and had hearing after hearing. Daisy had no memory of what took place when she was raped. Matthew Barnett, the boy who raped her, was from a well-known family. His grandfather was a former state representative and former sheriff. The interconnections of this family and the town didn't help Daisy's case. The court system dragged the case out for months before the charges against two of the boys were dropped. The prosecutor couldn't prove the allegations beyond a reasonable doubt. The boy who had raped Paige admitted to it and was charged.

After the charges were dropped, the rape became national news and another county stepped in to take a second look at the case. At the end of that investigation, there was enough evidence to charge Matthew Barnett with a second-degree count of endangering a child. There was insufficient evidence for sexual assault, so he just got probation.

## THE AUDRIE POTT COURT CASE

In the case of Audrie Pott, all three fifteen-year-old boys were convicted of possessing child pornography and committing sexual battery, with multiple felonies for each boy. One of the boys was sentenced to

After Audrie Pott's death, her parents filed a civil suit against her attackers. Here, her father and her stepmother appear at a 2013 news conference.

forty-five days in jail, while the other two were sentenced to thirty days each, served on weekends so that they wouldn't miss school. Audrie's parents filed a wrongful death suit, in which the boys had to take full responsibility for their actions and clear Audrie's name. The teens wrote a letter to her parents admitting guilt for what they had done and apologized.

# CHAPTER FIVE

# RECOVERY AFTER SEXUAL ASSAULT

S urvivors often struggle with returning to normal daily activities after an assault. The emotional and physical scars after sexual violence can deeply impact a person's ability to cope with academic, social, and personal responsibilities.

Victims often feel social pressure to act like everything is OK, regardless of what they feel inside. Survivors may know their attackers and can't avoid them if they have class together, live together, or work together. They may also have the same friends. They may try to sort out conflicting thoughts and feelings about their perpetrator if they knew them before the attack. This is a traumatic experience, and one common reaction is to try to forget the situation happened and move on.

## THE HEALING PROCESS

For survivors to go through the healing process, they must work with their physicians, counselors, and other

Healing is an essential process for survivors of sexual assault, even if it means temporarily stepping away from the stress of their daily lives.

caring adults and also take the appropriate time off from work, classes, and other academic responsibilities.

Each experience is different in how survivors will react after the assault.

According to CARDV, they may suppress the negative emotions they have after the attack or they can't focus on anything but the assault. Some change jobs, schools, or move as a way to cope with the incident. Others may withdraw from their social life to avoid dealing with confusing emotions and pain.

According to *Realities of Sexual Assault on Campus* by Best Colleges, these actions can help a survivor to move on after an assault:

# RAPE TRAUMA SYNDROME

According to the Center Against Rape & Domestic Violence (CARDV), the daily lives of sexual assault and rape survivors are forever changed both emotionally and physically. Symptoms of post-traumatic stress disorder (PTSD), also referred to as rape trauma syndrome, are often reported. According to CARDV, survivors can experience shock along with other emotional and physical distress, which may include:

- Fear
- Numbness
- Short-term memory loss
- Difficulty focusing
- Anxiety and/or depression
- Confusion/disorganization
- Sadness, rage, anger, and helplessness
- Guilt or belief that the assault was caused by the survivor's actions
- Embarrassment
- Insomnia/nightmares
- Flashbacks
- Denial
- Physical soreness or tension
- Feeling of self-harm, or suicide

**Make safe arrangements:** If you live with someone who has sexually assaulted you, have either dorm staff, the home of a trusted family member, or friends help you move to a new place. To stay safe, don't tell the offender about your new residence.

**Seek counseling:** If you are in college, the campus health office may help you find a sexual assault crisis counselor. The National Sexual Assault Hotline at 1-800-656-HOPE has counselors to talk with over the phone.

**File a civil protection order (CPO):** If you know the offender, you can get a protection order (restraining order). This court order is to keep the attacker away from you, and if he ignores a CPO, he can face criminal charges. The American Bar Association has sexual assault CPO procedures for all fifty states.

Over the long period of healing, sexual assault survivors may require the support of a counselor, friends, or family members.

# SURVIVORS BILL OF RIGHTS

In October 2016, President Obama signed into law a bill that provides specific rights to sexual assault survivors that are guaranteed regardless of whether they pursue legal action against their attackers. According to the Sexual Assault Survivors Rights Act, survivors have the right to be informed of these policies regarding:

- The right to not be charged fees for a sexual assault evidence collection kit (a rape kit)
- The right to have a sexual assault medical forensic examination regardless if charges are filed with law enforcement
- The right to be informed of results from rape kit testing that include a DNA profile match, toxicology report, or other information collected
- The right to be informed in writing of policies regarding the storage, preservation, and disposal of rape kits
- The right to be granted, upon written request, further preservation of rape kits or the evidence in them
- The right to have the availability of a sexual assault advocate, protective orders, and policies related to their enforcement
- The right to have the availability of victim compensation and restitution

**Additional healing actions:** Do whatever feels soothing or restoring to you, like taking walks and talking with friends who support you. If you feel stress then make changes to simplify your life.

## MOVING FORWARD

People's responses play a huge role in a survivor's decision on coming forward to report an assault. In the book *Campus Sexual Assault: College Women Respond* by Lauren Germain, survivors who sought out help from informal support providers like family and friends tended to receive positive reactions whereas ones that sought help from formal support providers tended to receive negative reactions. But there were a few who found counselors, faculty, and staff members to be very helpful.

## HEALING FOR DAISY COLEMAN

After four years of dealing with negative feelings of revenge, hate, and anger, Daisy Coleman wanted to forgive but not forget. "It's harder to live your life full of hate. I just want to move on," Daisy said in an interview in the Netflix documentary *Audrie & Daisy*.

Delaney Henderson, another rape survivor, reached out to Daisy and shared her story since they had similar experiences. Delaney never reported her assault because she was afraid. Eight months after Delaney's sexual assault, her rapist attacked another girl. She feels guilty for not helping get him off the street.

Daisy and Delaney share their stories with other victims to let them know they are not alone. Both girls were able to move on by supporting each other and by raising awareness about sexual assault. They also urge others to stand up to sexual violence. Survivors can heal, too, while helping others by participating in independent or collective actions that are social, political, or spiritual. These include organizing events for the community, speaking or presenting at awareness events, researching gender violence, serving in organizations to support other students, teaching self-defense classes, and working one-on-one with peers who have experienced sexual violence.

The Netflix original documentary, *Audrie & Daisy*, was released in September 2016 to critical acclaim.

## ORGANIZATIONS FOR SURVIVORS TO NETWORK

There are organizations across the country that survivors can go to for help and also participate in to help others. By sharing their experiences, survivors have healed.

## AFTER SILENCE

After Silence is an online support group for rape, sexual assault, and sexual abuse survivors. This support community helps victims recover by communicating with other survivors. They believe the first step to recovery is breaking the silence. Their mission is to provide a safe, loving,

Actress Christina Ricci and RAINN president Scott Berkowitz attend an event in Beverly Hills in 2011.

and thought-provoking support group for survivors of rape and sexual abuse.

## RAINN

RAINN (Rape, Abuse & Incest National Network) is the nation's largest anti–sexual violence organization, which created and operates the National Sexual Assault Hotline (800-656-HOPE) and the DOD Safe Helpline for the Department of Defense. It works with over one thousand local sexual assault service providers across the United States.

RAINN carries out programs to prevent sexual violence, help victims, and ensure that perpetrators are brought to justice. On its website at www.rainn.org, there are opportunities for survivors to share their experiences. You can help change the way people think about and respond to sexual violence. RAINN Speakers Bureau connects survivors with opportunities to share their stories and educate the public through speaking events and media interviews.

**advocate**  A person who informally represents a victim or survivor in the prosecution/disciplinary process.

**anxiety**  Fearful concern or an overwhelming sense of apprehension or fear.

**assailant**  A person who violently attacks another person.

**coerce**  To dominate another person by force.

**counselor**  A person who gives advice or counseling; this is especially helpful in court.

**deposition**  Testimony that is taken in writing under oath in court.

**DNA evidence**  Biological evidence that is a type of physical evidence to connect someone to a crime. Hair and body fluids are two examples.

**emergency contraception**  Pills that prevent pregnancy after a rape; morning-after pill.

**GHB**  A central nervous system depressant that is commonly referred to as a club drug and is used at bars, parties, clubs, and raves (all-night dance parties); street name is Ecstasy.

**incest**  Sexual intercourse between persons that are related and would be forbidden by law to marry.

**ketamine**  Drug that can cause hallucinations, reduce physical sensation, and induce temporary paralysis; also called Special K.

**marital rape**  Nonconsensual or forced sex in which the attacker is the victim's spouse.

**neurobiological condition** A medical condition that deals with the anatomy, physiology, and pathology of the nervous system.

**penetration** The insertion of a body part or other object into a vagina, anus, or mouth.

**perpetrator** A person who commits a crime.

**pervasive** Describes unwanted behavior that spreads.

**psychiatric examination** A history and mental status or exam done by a psychiatrist.

**PTSD (post-traumatic stress disorder)** A psychological reaction that occurs after a stressful or violent event, often causing the victim to mentally relive the experience. It can be triggered by sensory experiences of a smell, a sound, or a place.

**rape** Forcing someone to have sexual intercourse; forcibly penetrating someone's vagina or anus or causing that person to penetrate herself or himself, against the person's will.

**restraining order** A protective order used by the court to protect a person in a situation involving domestic violence, harassment, stalking, or sexual assault.

**restitution** Compensation to a victim for his or her losses.

**Rohypnol** Also known as forget me drug, roofie, and roach, a drug that has similar properties as valium. It can produce a strong amnesia effect so the victim may have limited or no recollection of a sexual assault.

**sodomy** Anal or oral sex between people.

**STD testing** Medical testing or screens done to see if sexually transmitted diseases were transferred from one person to another. This includes infections and HIV test.

Center Against Rape & Domestic Violence (CARDV)
Advocacy Center
2208 SW 3rd Street
Corvallis, OR 97333
(541) 738-8319
Website: http://cardv.org
Facebook: @CARDV
Twitter: @CARDV
CARDV provides services and support to those affected
by sexual and domestic violence and provides
leadership and education within the community to
change the societal conditions that cultivate these
forms of violence.

Feminist Majority Foundation (FMF)
1600 Wilson Boulevard, Suite 801
Arlington, VA 22209
(703) 522-2214
Website: http://www.feminist.org
Twitter: @feministnews
FMF was created to develop bold new strategies and
programs to advance women's equality, nonvio-
lence, and economic development, and to empower
women and girls in all sectors of society.

National Organization of Sisters of Color Ending Sexual
Assault (SCESA)
PO Box 625
Canton, CT 06019

Website: http://Sisterslead.org
Facebook: @SCESA
Twitter: @SCESA_WOC
The National Organization of Sisters of Color Ending
Sexual Assault is an advocacy organization dedicated to working with communities to create a just
society in which all women of color are able to live
healthy lives free of violence. Its purpose is to give
voice and develop action strategies that incorporate
and address the experiences and realities of women
of color in their communities.

National Sexual Violence Resource Center (NSVRC)
123 North Enola Drive
Enola, PA 17025
(717) 909-0710
Website: http://www.nsvrc.org
Facebook: @NSVRC
Twitter: @NSVRC
NSVRC's mission is to provide leadership in prevent-
ing and responding to sexual violence through
collaboration, sharing and creating resources, and
promoting research.

Rape, Abuse & Incest National Network (RAINN)
1220 L Street NW, Suite 505
Washington, DC 20005
(800) 656-HOPE (4673)
Website: https://www.rainn.org
Facebook: @rainn01
Twitter: @rainn01

Pinterest: @rainn01
Youtube: @RAINN01
RAINN is the nation's largest anti–sexual violence organization. RAINN created and operates the National Sexual Assault Hotline in partnership with more than one thousand local sexual assault service providers across the country and operates the DOD Safe Helpline for the Department of Defense.

Sex Information & Education Council of Canada (Sieccan)
235 Danforth Avenue, Suite 400
Toronto, ON MAK 1N2
Canada
(416) 466-5304
Website: http://www.sieccan.org
Sieccan works with health professionals, educators, and community organizations to ensure all Canadians have access to quality sexual health information, education, and related health and social services.

Sexual Assault Services of Saskatchewan (SASS)
103 – 1102 8th Avenue
Regina, SK S4R 1CR
Canada
(306) 757-1941
SASS supports agencies that offer services to survivors of sexual assault and abuse and provides a voice for prevention of sexual violence through awareness and education.

Vancouver Rape Relief and Women's Shelter
1424 Commercial Drive
Vancouver, BC V5L 5G2
Canada
(604) 872-8212
Website: https://www.rapereliefshelter.bc.ca
Vancouver Rape Relief and Women's Shelter is committed to advocating for women's equality. Its center works as an active force dedicated to challenge the social attitudes, laws, and institutional procedures that perpetuate male violence against women and children.

## WEBSITES

Because of the changing nature of internet links, Rosen Publishing has developed an online list of websites related to the subject of this book. This site is updated regularly. Please use this link to access the list:

http://www.rosenlinks.com/NTKL/Assault

# FOR FURTHER READING

Clark, Annie E., and Andrea L. Pino. *We Believe You: Survivors of Campus Sexual Assault.* New York, NY: Henry Holt & Co., 2016.

Eldridge, Alison, and Stephen Eldridge. *Investigate Club Drugs* (Investigate Drugs). New York, NY: Enslow Publishing, 2014.

Feinstein, Stephen. *Do You Wonder About Sex and Sexuality* (Got Issues). New York, NY: Enslow Publishing, 2015.

Kaplan, Arie. *A Young Man's Guide to Contemporary Issues* (Dating & Relationships).New York, NY: Rosen Publishing, 2012.

Lily, Henrietta. *Teen Mental Health* (Dating Violence). New York, NY: Rosen Publishing, 2012.

Lohmann, Raychelle Cassada and Sheela Raja. *The Sexual Trauma Workbook for Teen Girls: A Guide to Recovery from Sexual Assault and Abuse.* Oakland, CA: Instant Help Books, 2016.

*Sexting* (At Issue: Social Issues). New York, NY: Greenhaven Press, 2015.

*Sexual Assault on Campus* (Opposing Viewpoints). New York, NY: Greenhaven Press, 2016.

*Sexual Assault and the Military* (At Issue: Social Issues). New York, NY: Greenhaven Press, 2015.

*Sexual Violence* (Opposing Viewpoints). New York, NY: Greenhaven Press, 2014.

*Violence Against Women* (Current Controversies). New York, NY: Greenhaven Press, 2016.

*Audrie & Daisy* (documentary). Directed by Bonni Cohen and Jon Shenk. Netflix Documentary, September 2016.

Bergland, Christopher. "Neuroscientists Discover the Roots of 'Fear-Evoked Freezing.'" *Psychology Today*, May 1, 2014. https://www.psychologytoday.com /blog/the-athletes-way/201405/neuroscientists -discover-the-roots-fear-evoked-freezing.

Best College. "The Realities of Sexual Assault on Campus." 2017. http://www.bestcolleges.com/resources /preventing-sexual-assault.

Georgetown Law. "Myths and Facts About Sexual Violence." Retrieved January 17, 2017. https://www.law .georgetown.edu/campus-life/advising-counseling /personal-counseling/sarvl/general-information.cfm.

Germain, Lauren J. *Campus Sexual Assault: College Women Respond.* Baltimore, MD: Johns Hopkins University Press, 2016.

Gray, Robin Hattersley. "Sexual Assault Statistics." *Campus Safety*, March 5, 2012. http://www .campussafetymagazine.com/article/Sexual -Assault-Statistics-and-Myths.

Grinberg, Emmanuella, and Catherine E. Shoichet. "Brock Turner Released from Jail After Serving 3 Months for Sexual Assault." CNN, September 2, 2016. http://www .cnn.com/2016/09/02/us/brock-turner-release-jail/.

Know Your IX. "Why Schools Handle Sexual Violence Reports." Retrieved January 31, 2017. http:// knowyourix.org/why-schools-handle-sexual

-violence-reports/.

National Institute on Alcohol Abuse and Alcoholism. "College Drinking." Retrieved May 9, 2017. https://www.niaaa.nih.gov/search/site/college%2520drinking.

National Sexual Violence Resource Center. "False Reporting." 2012. http://www.nsvrc.org/sites/default/files/Publications_NSVRC_Overview_False-Reporting.pdf.

National Sexual Violence Resource Center. "Statistics About Sexual Violence." 2015. http://www.nsvcr.org/sites/default/files/publications.

RAINN. "Campus Sexual Violence: Statistics." Retrieved January 18, 2017. https://www.rainn.org/statistics/campus-sexual-violence.

RAINN. "Drug-Facilitated Sexual Assault." Retrieved February 11, 2017. https://www.rainn.org/articles/drug-facilitated-sexual-assault.

Reed, Tucker. "After Being Failed by My College's Administration, I Posted My Rapist's Name and Photo on the Internet." XOJane, April, 25, 2013. http://www.xojane.com/issues/tucker-reed-outs-rapist-at-usc.

Shaheen, Jeanne. "Sexual Assault Survivors Rights Act." October 2016.www.Shaheen.Senate.gov/imo/media/doc/2016-02-23.

Tesfaye, Sophia. "John Kasich's Casual Victim Blaming 'Advice': If You Don't Want to Be Raped, 'Don't Go to Parties Where There's a Lot of Alcohol.'" Salon, April 15, 2016. http://www.salon.com/2016/04/15/john_kasichs_casual_victim_blaming_advice_if_you_dont_want_to_be_raped_dont_go_to_parties_where_theres_a_lot_of_alcohol/.

# A

alcohol, 10–11, 13–14, 28

# C

campus authorities, 30–31
campus rape, 28
*Campus Sexual Assault*, 33, 50
CARDV (Center Against Rape
   & Domestic Violence), 46–47
civil protection order (CPO), 48
club drugs, 13
Coleman, Daisy, 24–25, 43, 50,
   51
colleges, 27–31, 36, 48
consent, 4, 9, 11, 13, 22
counselors, 30, 34, 38, 45, 48, 50
   sexual assault crisis, 48

# D

denial, 32, 47
depression, 21, 47
DNA evidence, 41
drug-facilitated sexual assault,
   13
drugs, 11, 13–14
   date rape, 13

# E

evidence, 26, 32, 40–43, 49

# F

fraternities, 28, 33

# G

guilt, 18, 44, 47

# H

harassment, 12

# L

law enforcement, 36, 40, 49

# M

marital rape, 9
media portrayal, 32
medical examinations, 39, 41
memories, 13–14, 24, 41, 43
military, 12, 16

# N

National Intimate Partner and
   Sexual Violence Survey, 17
National Sexual Assault Hotline,
   41, 48
NSVRC (National Sexual
   Violence Resource Center),
   40

## P

parties, 11, 20, 23, 33
personal space, 9, 18
physical evidence, 30, 32, 39
post-traumatic stress disorder (PTSD), 21, 47
Pott, Audrie, 23, 24, 43–44
pregnancy, 41
pressure, 9, 18, 25, 33

## R

RAINN (Rape, Abuse, and Incest National Network), 8, 13, 18–19, 52
RAINN statistics, 26, 29
rape, 6–10, 13, 15–16, 18, 22, 27–28, 31–33, 38, 40, 42–43, 51–52
  avoiding, 11
  crisis centers, 38
  date, 16
  false claims, 40
  kits, 11, 25–26, 32, 41, 49
  prevention program, 30
  prosecution, 37
  recovery, 45, 47, 49, 51
  revenge, 40, 50
  survivors, 47, 50
  trauma syndrome, 47
Rohypnol/roofies, 13–14

## S

sex discrimination, 29
sexting, non-mutual, 10
sexual assault
  CPO procedures, 48
  statistics, 28, 60
  survivors, 31, 36, 48–49
  what it is, 7–8
Survivors Rights Act, 49
sexual harassment, 10, 12, 29
shame, 8, 26
student victims, 26–27, 29, 31, 33, 35
suicide, 21, 47
survivors, 21, 26, 30–31, 34–35, 45–47, 49–52

## T

teens, 16, 24, 44
threats, 9, 25
  verbal, 7
Title IX, 27, 29
toxic masculinity, 7
transgender community, 18
trust, 16, 19–20

## V

victim blaming, 11
violence, domestic, 34

## ABOUT THE AUTHOR

Jeana Tetzlaff is an author of several short stories and articles as well as a contributor to the *Gladstone Dispatch*.

## PHOTO CREDITS

Cover Iakov Filimonov/Shutterstock.com; p. 5 Redchopsticks/Getty Images; pp. 7, 16, 26, 37, 45 pimchawee/Shutterstock.com; pp. 8, 20 PeopleImages/E+/Getty Images; p. 10 mother image/Taxi/Getty Images; p. 11 Scott Olson/Getty Images; p. 14 AFP/Getty Images; p. 17 Jupiter Images/Photolibrary/Getty Images; p. 22 Roy Morsch/Corbis/Getty Images; p. 23 © AP Images; p. 27 Hero Images/Getty Images; p. 29 Burger/Canopy/Getty Images; p. 38 Santa Clara County Sheriff via AP; p. 42 sturti/E+/Getty Images; p. 44 Robert Galbraith/Reuters/Newscom; p. 46 Michael Prince/Corbis/Getty Images; p. 48 Voisin/Phanie/Canopy/Getty Images; p. 51 Bloomberg/Getty Images; p. 52 Michael Kovac/WireImage/Getty Image

Design: Michael Moy; Layout: Tahara Anderson; Photo Researcher: Nicole Baker